Forge Ahead

by Joseph Lehmann
illustrated by B. Walker

Chapters

Harcourt

Orlando   Boston   Dallas   Chicago   San Diego

Visit *The Learning Site!*

www.harcourtschool.com

A Scene from the Past

The scene is a summer fair at a large city park. A line of children forms outside a booth. Other booths feature food, games, performers, or arts and crafts. None has a line as long as the one at Chris McFee's booth.

McFee is demonstrating the art of blacksmithing. In his booth is a portable forge. A forge is a small furnace used to heat metal. The fuel might be charcoal or coal.

McFee holds a small iron rod in the fire with a pair of tongs. The iron glows redder and redder as it heats up. McFee watches carefully. He must decide when the iron is hot enough to pound it into a different shape.

A volunteer pumps the bellows. The bellows blow air into the fire in the forge to make it burn hotter. Then McFee helps a boy beat the iron rod with a hammer. McFee is holding the rod down on a very strong metal "table" called an anvil.

Sparks fly as the boy pounds the rod. Then the metal hisses as McFee uses the tongs to plunge the rod into cold water. The rod is now a nail—made the old-fashioned way.

McFee gives the nail to the boy. He wants him to remember—and tell others—what a blacksmith does.

Chris McFee gives his demonstrations for fun and education. He is quick to tell you that he isn't really a blacksmith. He is an ornamental woodworker and carpenter in Langley, Washington. "About twenty years ago," he says, "I decided I wanted to make my own tools."

Until about 1900 most iron tools and hardware items were made by hand. Every American town and village had blacksmiths. (Think of how many people are named Smith!)

Long ago, blacksmiths were rugged men with strong arms and hands made hard by work. Their craft was highly respected. Henry Wadsworth Longfellow's poem "The Village Blacksmith" is one of many tributes to their skill.

Times Change

In the early 1900s, there was less need for the products made by blacksmiths. It had become easier for Americans to get factory-made hardware. This "store-bought" hardware was cheaper than handmade products.

As people began driving cars, they no longer needed horseshoes or wagon fittings. Ornamental iron fell out of fashion as a building material.

By 1940 few smiths were still working at their craft. "The village blacksmith" had passed into history.

During the 1960s, some Americans became interested in blacksmithing as an art or hobby. They would install a forge in a garage and try to make simple tools. The problem was finding people who could teach them.

Chris McFee was lucky to live where he did. In small towns in the West and South, blacksmithing had never quite died out. The old smiths there could teach new ones, as in the old days. A group called the NorthWest Blacksmith Association was formed to help support the blacksmiths' craft.

Tamar Kaufman was not so lucky. She grew up in Brooklyn, New York. She became interested in black-smithing through her love of horses. However, there were no blacksmiths in New York City to teach her the skill.

Kaufman went to a school for blacksmiths in Oklahoma. Then, with a friend, she started a business called Horseshoeing with a Woman's Touch. They traveled up and down the East Coast. They carried a portable blacksmith's shop in a pickup truck.

Blacksmiths Today

Most people today think the main work of black-smiths is making horseshoes. In fact, according to some smiths, horseshoeing isn't blacksmithing at all. People who make horseshoes are called farriers, not blacksmiths.

When people see a blacksmith at work, they are often surprised at the variety of products produced by this rugged craft.

Blacksmiths today make handsome handcrafted tools. They make elegant furniture, lamps, and other household items. They make toys and jewelry. They make decorative iron gates and railings for homes. They also make steel sculptures that stand in front of office buildings.

Phill Baldwin was fascinated by his introduction to the blacksmith's craft. As a child he saw a demonstration much like Chris McFee's. Later he found an old forge at his school. He talked a teacher into letting him try it out.

Baldwin went on to build his own forge and install it in a New York City junk shop. He spent ten years learning to be a blacksmith by trial and error.

Today Baldwin is known for his handcrafted knives. Tributes to his work come from around the world. Baldwin also teaches a course for beginners at the Penland School of Crafts in North Carolina. In two weeks his students learn to make all the basic tools that blacksmiths use.

That doesn't make them blacksmiths, however. In earlier days a smith spent three to seven years learning the craft. After eight to ten years of work, he could call himself a "master blacksmith."

The Skill of Blacksmithing

There is more to blacksmithing than beating hot iron with a hammer. Blacksmithing takes exact timing and a careful set of steps. One wrong blow can ruin hours of work.

Blacksmiths must be able to tell how hot the metal is just by looking at it. They must know when and where to strike. They must understand different kinds of iron and steel and the materials that are mixed with them. They must know how the heated metal will behave when hammered.

Blacksmiths learn many ways to change the shape of heated iron. For example, they can make an iron bar thicker and shorter by hitting the end of it. They can make it narrower by hammering the sides of it.

They can even bend a heated bar into a curved shape. They do this by hammering the bar around a curved form. Blacksmiths can also weld iron bars together. They can punch small holes in the hot iron. They can cut out larger holes.

A skilled blacksmith can create a very delicate pattern. It might even look like lace from a distance. However, iron is much, much stronger than lace.

Younger blacksmiths today think of themselves as artists. Some have been to art school. Many are members of the ABANA—the Artist-Blacksmith's Association of North America. This group was started in 1973. That year a group of blacksmiths met in Lumpkin, Georgia. The younger smiths wanted to learn some tips from the older smiths.

The smiths had such a good time exchanging ideas that they decided to form an organization. Their goal was to preserve a special skill from the past. They wanted to make sure this skill, this art form, was not forgotten in the future.

The first blacksmith to officially join the group was a man in his 70s. As a "village smith," he had shoed mules and repaired metal wagon wheels. He was thrilled that young people wanted to learn this skill.

Forty-seven people attended that first meeting in 1973. Today the ABANA has more than 2,250 members on five continents. They are happy to report that every year more schools and workshops teach blacksmithing. This skill is here to stay.

Did the village blacksmith of the past think of himself as an artist? Probably not, because his was a much-needed and valued trade. "Art" was something for museums, wealthy customers, and spare time.

However, when you add imagination to skill, art is what you often get. We see it in the work of master smiths of earlier times. We see it too in the work of today's blacksmiths who are learning from the masters' work.